The Culturally Curious

A Traveler's Primer for Global Connections

Table of Contents

The world is a book and those who do not travel
read only one page.

Chapter 1. Introduction

Immerse yourself in an enthralling journey around the world with our Special Report: "The Culturally Curious: A Traveler's Primer for Global Connections". This report serves as your golden ticket, unlocking the vibrant tapestry of global cultures, hidden gems, and diverse traditions that the world has to offer. Helping you navigate through the labyrinth of societal norms, languages, cuisines, and hidden local secrets, this report aims to transform you from a bystander to an active participant in unique cultural experiences - making travel more meaningful. This joyous reading expedition not only broadens your understanding of the world but leaves you with a desire to embark on your own global adventure. So, get ready to gain a fresh perspective on travel and the art of making indelible connections. This report isn't just a purchase; it's your passport to the world! Buckle up and prepare for a journey of a lifetime!

Chapter 2. Unraveling the Fascination of Travel

The concept of travel carries with it an inexplicable charm, an inherent fascination that feels almost magical. The allure of exploration, the thirst for adventure, the empathy that springs from shared cultural experiences – every aspect of travel tells a story that is as enchanting as it is broadening. When we talk about travel, we're not merely discussing the act of moving from one geographical location to another. Instead, we're delving into an insightful exploration of cultures, traditions, cuisines, languages, and the endless wonders that the world has to offer.

2.1. The Allure of Exploration

Journeying to new places has always been a fundamental part of the human experience - it's interwoven into the very fabric of our existence. It is no surprise then that exploration is, in essence, a deeply ingrained part of our psyche. Since time immemorial, humans have been natural explorers, venturing into unknown territories, pushing geographical boundaries, understanding—and often shaping—the world around them. Be it ancient civilizations navigating the vast expanse of the seas to trade or discover new lands, or modern-day globe-trotters scouting out the remote corners of the world for unique experiences; the allure of exploration acts as a powerful motivator, propelling us into new dimensions of experiences and identity formation.

2.2. The Advent of Adventurous Travel

The onset of adventure travel has brought with it a realm of experiences previously unimaginable in the scope of traditional excursion. By its very nature, it pushes the boundaries of what one can achieve and experience, providing a heady mix of thrill, challenge, and self-discovery. Adventure travel is not simply about physically challenging activities; more often than not, it also incorporates exploration of remote areas, encountering wildlife, and engaging with the local cultures—all adding to the enthralling mystique of travel. Pushing your boundaries, testing your limits, and experiencing the exuberant joy of success or the humble acceptance of failure, adventurous travel has a life-altering quality that is profoundly enriching in its impact.

2.3. The Empathy Evoked through Cultural Engagement

Embracing the cultural facet of regions visited is an integral part of discerning why travel fascinates us so. Engaging with local cultures, traditions, and communities is not merely a captivating experience; it is also a way to foster empathy and mutual understanding among diverse societies. As travelers immerse themselves in local living, they usually experience an enhanced understanding and appreciation for not just the differences, but also the shared aspects of the human experience—echoing the sentiment of unity in diversity.

2.4. The Awakening of the Senses

Travel offers a palette of experiences that tantalize our senses. From the aromatic scent of colorful, bustling spice markets to the soothing melody of language unfamiliar to our ears, every place visited presents a symphony of sensory experiences that leave a lasting imprint on our memory. These sensory experiences not only enhance our understanding and enjoyment of the places we visit, they also heighten our awareness and appreciation for the vast and diverse world we inhabit.

2.5. Discovering One's "Self"

Amidst the hustle and bustle of everyday life, we often forget the urgency of self-introspection. Introspection and self-discovery become poignant during travels, as one steps away from the familiar surroundings and everyday routines. Travel is often seen as a solitary journey, even when you're not technically alone. It's a quest within, an exploration of one's deepest desires, apprehensions, dreams, and perspectives. It's about uncovering the layers of your own personality, about confronting the parts of your "self" that remain obscured in daily living. This facet of travel is a fascinating and rewarding journey within yourself.

2.6. Beyond the Borders: Breaking down Stereotypes

Travel allows us to break through the invisible walls built by societal norms, regularity, and routine. These newly encountered perspectives often work towards shattering stereotypical viewpoints, enhancing our understanding of the world and its diverse cultures. We often come to realize that while some cultural nuances are unique to specific regions, at the heart of it all, people everywhere share common dreams, hopes, and challenges. This shattering of stereotypes and broadening of perspectives adds to the enchanting allure of travel.

In conclusion, the fascination associated with travel is a cumulative outcome of numerous elements—adventure, exploration, cultural engagement, sensory delight, self-discovery, and the breaking down of stereotypes. These elements intertwine to provide a diverse and vibrant array of experiences that inspire, educate, and encourage personal growth. The allure of travel, therefore, lies not only in the physical journey from one place to another but more profoundly, in the emotional, intellectual, and spiritual journeys that illuminate our understanding of ourselves and the world that we're a part of. The fascination of travel indeed holds in its grasp an unparalleled charm, subjectively reshaping our worldview, leaving us with a thirst for more.

Chapter 3. The Art of Embracing Cultural Differences

In any journey, stepping off the familiar path is both a courageous and rewarding act. It demands us to be open, to embrace the unknown, and to celebrate the intriguing cacophony of human diversity. But how do we facilitate this process? How can we truly immerse ourselves in diverse cultures? One must first understand and acknowledge cultural differences. It's less about examining these differences under a microscope and more about experiencing them, engaging with them, and ultimately, finding beauty in them.

3.1. Unveiling the Veil of Otherness

Our perception of 'otherness' often stems from a lack of understanding. When we encounter cultural customs, practices, or ideologies that are foreign to us, it can become easy to label them as 'strange' or 'different'. However, such labels only serve to distance us from our goal of cultural immersion and understanding. We must instead embrace these differences, not as barriers but as opportunities for profound learning. Remember, cultural differences are not hurdles, but steps towards a more inclusive, harmonious world.

3.2. Dialogue Over Debate

Far too often we view our interactions through the lens of a debate, a win-or-lose proposition. However, when it comes to culture, we must replace this mindset with one of dialogue. A dialogue means listening with sincere interest, presenting our points with humility and empathy, and being open to new insights and perspectives. It is a dynamic interchange of ideas that fosters mutual respect and sets the stage for genuine bonds to form.

3.3. Reveling in the Spectrum of Human Expressions

Art, music, dance, cuisine, clothing, festivals - these are all manifestations of a culture's unique expression. Each one is a glorious revelation of the human spirit; an insight into the hopes, dreams, and stories that are woven into the very fabric of that culture. To embrace cultural differences, we must not only appreciate these modes of expression but revel in them. Participate in regional dances, wear native clothing, relish local delicacies - become an active participant in these festivals of human creativity.

3.4. The Universality of Human Values

Despite our varied cultural backgrounds, at our core, we all share a set of common human values - compassion, honest communication, respect for each other's dignity, and a desire for harmonious living. Recognizing these shared values can serve as a bridge, connecting us across cultural boundaries. We should not allow cultural differences to distract us from the universality of our basic human nature.

3.5. Letting Go of Prejudices

Prejudices act like dirty lenses, distorting our view of reality. They can prevent us from seeing the beauty that lies in cultural differences. Letting go of these biases is not always easy, but it is essential for genuine cultural immersion. Question your beliefs, challenge your assumptions, and, above all, be willing to learn and change.

3.6. A Dose of Humility

Embracing cultural differences also calls for a generous dose of humility. As we venture into unfamiliar cultural terrains, we must refrain from judgment and approach each experience with an open and humble mind. There will be practices that we may not immediately understand or agree with. In these instances, remember that our perspective is not the only one and that our way of life is not the only way.

In conclusion, the art of embracing cultural differences hinges upon our will to understand, our ability to accept, and our courage to broaden our perspective. Immerse yourself wholeheartedly in this splendiferous diversity, as it is one of the most enriching gifts that travel has to offer.

Chapter 4. Language: The Bridge to Mutual Understanding

Language is deemed indispensable in the art of human interaction. It is our primary medium for communication, a vital key to understanding and a bridge that facilitates mutual understanding and transcends borders. Language gravitates people towards commonality, which encourages companionship and establishes connections.

4.1. Value of Language in Travel

The role of language in travel is tremendously vital. It is imperative that you, as a traveler, appreciate its importance. It forms part of the pathway you embark on as you tread unfamiliar territories. Learning the local language can significantly enhance your travel experience. Fundamentally, it is a tool that facilitates communication, but when you dive deeper, you come to realize that language is the core nexus between you and the host culture.

Learning a few phrases in the local tongue can aid tremendously in breaking the ice, showing respect to your hosts, and navigating your way around. Fundamentally, language serves as an essential tool in fostering multinational dialogue, building lifelong relationships, and exploring cultural nuances that make each destination unique. Furthermore, every language has its phrases, idioms, and words that vanquish translation, embodying certain aspects of a country's culture and encapsulating its essence in ways that are often deeply insightful and emotionally bonding.

4.2. The Intricacies of Language

Every dialect, every syntax, every word in any given language holds a story. The language reflects the history, culture, and personality of the people speaking it, painted through the unique color palette of indigenous metaphors and slang. The emotion that certain combinations of words can elicit can rarely be replicated in another language. The way languages incorporate feelings and emotions gracefully elevates their beauty and further augments their potential to facilitate mutual understanding.

The immense diversity that languages present is a testament to the considerable variety of ideas and perspectives across different cultures. It is due to this magnificent kaleidoscope of linguistic diversity that we have, as a collective, been able to generate remarkably vibrant societies, civilizations, ideologies, and intellectual traditions.

4.3. Learning New Languages: An Act of Cultural Empathy

Initiating steps towards learning a new language is an act of empathizing with the culture one is about to encounter. It promotes cultural immersion: the process of becoming deeply involved or absorbed in a particular culture, to the extent that one begins to comprehend and appreciate it from an internal perspective rather than from an external, possibly exoticized perspective.

Language learning should not be driven by the aspiration of attaining fluency or nearing perfection but by an ethos of respect for the host community, curiosity for its cultural subtleties, and a desire to understand and connect on a deeper level. Make no mistake, as linguistic competence increases, so does one's confidence to venture further, to dive deeper, and to let serendipity guide one's journey.

4.4. Encountering Language Barriers: A Cross-cultural Puzzle

Travel invariably involves confronting and managing language barriers. These encounters should not be seen as obstacles, but rather as opportunities to enhance understanding, lend an ear to the silent language of gestures and body language, and feel a sense of humor at shared bewilderment over complex linguistic knots.

Often, it's these seemingly challenging experiences that end up being the most enriching and memorable moments of one's travel. They not only provide a channel for self-growth but also invite you to think of creative ways to express yourself beyond the conventional contours of your native language.

4.5. Words as Souvenirs: Collecting Linguistic Gems

As you navigate through the various corners of the world, consider each learned word or phrase as a precious souvenir that you take back with you. These linguistic gems will serve as eternal reminders of those cherished moments, the conversations you had, and the relationships you forged.

The act of collecting linguistic gems will not only enrich your cultural experience but will also allow you to draw bridges to other cultures that share common words or linguistic roots. These commonalities might inspire you towards exciting new paths of exploration and understanding.

In conclusion, language, in its diverse expressions, holds enormous potential to serve as a bridge to mutual understanding. It invites you to explore unfamiliar terrains, discover new signifies of expression, empathize with local experiences, and ultimately, celebrate the incredible diversity of global communication. As you pack your suitcase for your next adventure, remember to pack a thirst for linguistic knowledge, a puzzle-solving mindset for language barriers, and an empty jar for collecting linguistic souvenirs.

Chapter 5. Celebrating Traditions: Festivals Around the World

Understanding the world is like unraveling a prodigious puzzle where there are countless, intricately woven threads for us to explore. One such crucial thread is the awe-inspiring range of festivals celebrated around the world. Festivals act as a vibrant frame, capturing the essence of a place's culture, traditions, history, and community spirit. This chapter delves into various global festivals, guiding you to meaningful encounters with humanity's rich and diverse cultural tapestry.

5.1. Communal Celebrations: The Heartbeat of Societies

Festivals are a manifestation of our shared human ethos - they serve as milestones on the calendar, beckoning everyone to pause, celebrate, and come together. Long before calendars, festivals were nature's way of marking the passing of seasons, instructing societies when to sow and when to reap. Today, these communal celebrations are not just about religious observances or historical commemorations, but are also entangled with our collective identity, social structure, and shared values.

From the vibrant colors of India's Holi to the grand parade of Brazil's Carnival, each festival carries a unique rhythm and spirit, often steeped in centuries-old customs and traditions. These events offer a captivating lens through which visitors can connect with the local culture on a deeper level, beyond the veneer of the everyday.

5.2. Witnessing Humanity's Palette: Faith, History, and Identity

The range of global festivals can be mind-boggling yet exhilarating. Each celebration echoes an undercurrent of collective history, faith, and identity. Born out of a region's past, the festivals help to shape its present and future while adroitly reflecting the values of its people.

Milford's Festival of Lanterns in New Zealand, for instance, is deeply rooted in the celebration of Matariki, the Maori New Year. It is an homage beloved by all Kiwis, illuminating the depths of the indigenous Maori heritage blended with contemporary New Zealand society. Similarly, Día de los Muertos (Day of the Dead) in Mexico is a poignant Mexican celebration aimed at honoring and remembering the departed, integrating prehispanic rituals with Catholic beliefs.

Festivals thus become a living tableau of human history and faith, providing a deeper understanding of the global community.

5.3. A Gastronomical Journey through Festivals

A key aspect of many festivals worldwide is the triumphant celebration of food. Special dishes and drinks often seen during festivals provide the perfect accompaniment to the revelry - they are the shared ingredients spread across the global pantry, which leaves a lasting impression on our mind and palate.

During the Chinese New Year, you will find tables laden with long noodles symbolizing longevity, while the Scottish Hogmanay showcases an ancestral tradition of 'first-footing' where a gift of whisky and black bun - a rich, dried fruit pastry - is given for good luck. Each food ritual marries tradition with taste, providing a holistic experience that tantalizes all your senses.

5.4. Lessons in Empathy and Perspective: The Festival Way

Perhaps one of the essential takeaways from celebrating or observing global festivals is newfound empathy and perspective. Witnessing and participating in these communal events allow you to walk a mile in someone else's shoes, if only for a day.

Whether it's watching the sheer emotional power of Spain's Semana Santa (Holy Week), participating in Japan's vibrant Obon Festival or marveling at the silent prayers floating skywards during Thailand's Yi Peng Lantern Festival; these experiences teach us to appreciate the world's diversity. More than just a celebration, these festivals are a lesson in empathy, helping us step back from our sometimes restrictive perspectives and immerse ourselves in the rich body of human experience.

In summation, festivals around the world offer a doorway to cultural understanding and human connection. Engaging with these diverse celebrations enhances our comprehension of how societies function, enjoy, and rise above everyday life to honor traditions, beliefs, and the undying spirit of community. They serve as a reminder that no matter how different our cultures may be, we are intrinsically bound by our shared laughter, tears, celebration, and our collective stride towards the future. It is in these vibrant intersections of shared human experiences that we find genuine connections and gratifying travel experiences.

In the ensuing chapters, we will extend this exploration of global connections to other intriguing realms, such as language, food, and social norms, further enriching your understanding of the beauty and complexity of our world. Through this journey, our hope is to inspire more than just your wanderlust - we aim to kindle your curiosity for deeper, more meaningful travel encounters.

Chapter 6. Savoring the Palette of Global Cuisine

One of the most riveting aspects of travel is undoubtedly the opportunity to immerse oneself in the exotic and sometimes unfamiliar tastes that different global cuisines offer. Engaging with the local cuisine is not simply about satisfying hunger or thirst, it's about diving headfirst into the heart of the culture, imbibing its traditions, and savoring its flavors with each bite and sip.

6.1. The Role of Food in Culture

Food is an integral part of a culture's identity. It represents the history, geography, and spirit of a region, forged over centuries. Historically, what communities ate was determined by what the land could produce. Through ingenuity and tradition, culinary cultures evolved to reflect the abundance, scarcity, or adaptability of these local resources. As societies modernized, and globalization interconnected the world, new ingredients found their way onto plates, and new adaptations of traditional recipes were born. Today, trying a national dish or a regional specialty becomes a way of tasting local history and experiencing a piece of the culture.

6.2. Understanding the Global Food Map

The world's cuisines are incredibly diverse and rich, each one distinct yet linked through a complex web of historical, geographical, and social ties. Let's embark on a virtual culinary journey across different continents.

The Americas, both North and South, offer a vast range of cuisines.

From the deep, smoky flavors of Southern barbeque to the fiery stews of Mexico, from the unique piquancy of Peruvian ceviche to the iconic burgers of the US, this region is marked by a lively blend of Native American, African, European and Asian influences.

European cuisine is equally diverse, with Mediterranean diets relying heavily on fresh, local ingredients like olive oil, seafood, and plentiful produce. In contrast, Northern European countries traditionally employed cooking methods such as smoking, pickling, and preserving to withstand long, harsh winters.

Asia is a powerhouse of flavor, boasting an incredible variety of foods. Be it the kick of spices in Indian curries, the balance of flavors in Thai dishes, the freshness of Vietnamese cuisine, or the delicate precision of Japanese sushi, every gastronomic experience here tells a different story.

Africa's culinary scene is a vibrant yet underexplored mosaic of flavors, reflecting a variety of cultures, tribes, and traditions. From the hearty tagines of Morocco to the spicy, meaty braais of South Africa, from the comforting jollof rice in West Africa to the tangy injera bread in Ethiopia, food is a way of life in Africa.

6.3. Adventurous Eats: Pushing the Bounditarian Cuisine

For those with a bold palate, venturing into unusual or 'exotic' culinary territory can be an exhilarating part of one's journey. Tasting the snake wine in Vietnam or munching on fried tarantulas in Cambodia, or gorging on Hákarl (fermented shark) in Iceland is not only a potentially challenging culinary adventure but also an insight into the culinary extremes that different cultures can encompass.

6.4. Street Food: The Heart of Local Cuisine

Street food is often the most honest expression of a place's culinary soul. It's accessible, inexpensive, and has a unique way of showcasing local flavors and cooking techniques. Some global street food champions include Thailand's Pad Thai, Mexico's Tacos, India's Chaats, to name a few. Each of these foods tell a tale of their place of origin and their people - stories that entice, engage, and enrich the travelers' culinary catalog.

6.5. Cooking Classes & Food Tours: A Step Further

Going beyond just tasting new dishes, cooking classes and food tours enable travelers to delve deeper into the culinary tradition of a place. Cooking classes offer hands-on experiences, learning from local chefs, involving one's senses to build a deeper understanding of the local culture. Food tours typically encompass sampling a variety of dishes, visits to local markets, or even joining a family meal. It can be a thrilling and deeply immersive opportunity to learn, eat, and celebrate the global tapestry of cuisines.

6.6. Responsible Culinary Experiences

As we surrender ourselves to the delight of global cuisines, it's crucial to approach this exploration responsibly. Supporting local eateries instead of global food chains, respecting local gastronomic traditions, reducing waste, and making environmentally conscious food choices can go a long way in ensuring our culinary adventures do not come at the expense of our host cultures and environments.

In conclusion, as you explore the world, remember that behind each ingredient there is a farmer, behind each dish there is a cook, and behind each meal there is a story. So whether you are savoring the warm, hearty stews of the Scottish Highlands, relishing the bright, vibrant flavors of Peruvian ceviche, or crunching into the crispy, buzzing treats of Beijing's street markets, remember to savor and celebrate the cultures, the people, and the stories you encounter along your culinary journey. For it is through these experiences, these connections, that travel, and indeed eating, can truly transform us. Savoring the palette of global cuisine is, after all, a feast for not just our taste buds, but also for our soul.

Chapter 7. Must-Visit Hidden Gems of Each Continent

As we venture into the exploration of uncharted territories that dot the world, we realize that each continent hides a kaleidoscopic plethora of untapped beauties in its corners, often beyond the reach of the general tourist crowd and routine travel guides. It's these unspoiled, quaint places, brimming with character and teeming with local charm, that paint an authentic picture of a region's cultural landscape. As you wander through these paths less traveled, yield to the allure of exploration —the thrill of discovering hidden gems that make each journey monumental and unique. Get ready to dive into the lesser-known wonders that each continent cherishes in its folds, from the secluded beaches of Australia to the ethereal Northern lights of Antarctica.

7.1. Australia & Oceania: The Secluded Shores

Beginning our journey in the heart of the Southern continent, we weave our way through the less explored Australian terrain. One can't help but be enamored by Fraser Island, the largest sand island globally, lying off the Queensland coast. With its shimmering sand dunes, ancient rainforests, and mirror-like freshwater lakes, it offers a respite away from the cities' chaos. In New Zealand, the Waitomo Glowworm Caves hold a mesmerizing secret. These caves, millions of years old, are adorned with thousands of glowworms, illuminating the dark interiors with a surreal, starry ambiance.

7.2. Asia: Harmony of Tradition and Modernity

Asia, a melting pot of diverse cultures, traditions, and histories, is home to countless unexplored corners. In India, tucked away in the verdant hills of Meghalaya, lies Mawlynnong—declared the cleanest village in Asia. This paradise showcases the harmony between humans and nature, with its well-maintained gardens, meticulously clean lanes, and living root bridges. Meanwhile, on the Japanese island of Hokkaido, an out-of-the-ordinary spectacle awaits visitors in the town of Biei— the Patchwork Road and Panorama Road. These scenic routes are known for their picturesque landscapes that change colors with the seasons.

7.3. Africa: Echoes of Untamed Wilderness

In the heart of Africa, Ghana's stilt village of Nzulezo, built over Lake Tadane, is stunning testimony to human adaptation to the natural environment. With less crowded Safari experiences – like the Selous Game reserve in Tanzania – Africa offers a truly intimate encounter with the untamed wilderness, away from the beaten path.

7.4. Europe: Offbeat Extravaganza

Europe's immense cultural wealth often eclipses lesser-known spots. Like Italy's Alberobello, with its distinctive Trulli houses, and Poland's Wrocław, home to hundreds of miniature gnome statues, each telling a slice of the city's history. In Scotland, the Isle of Staffa offers an unusual sight with its hexagonal basalt columns, harking back to Ireland's famous Giant's Causeway.

7.5. North America: Chronicles of Resilient Ruins

North America's hidden gems give us a peek into the intriguing confluence of the old and new, with Mayan Ruins like Calakmul in Mexico presenting a stark contrast to the modernization seen in the cities. In Canada, the historic town of Lunenburg, Nova Scotia holds the reputation for being the best surviving British colonial town in North America.

7.6. South America: Secrets of Old Worlds

South America, laden with ancient civilization traces, also hides cities less explored. Brazil's Lençóis Maranhenses National Park, with its cascading white sand dunes and seasonal rainwater lagoons, is a visual spectacle. The argentine ghost town of Epecuén, once a thriving spa retreat before being flooded and then abandoned, adds a hauntingly beautiful layer to the continent's tale.

7.7. Antarctica: A Polar Paradise

Journeying to the icy realms of Antarctica, we come across the sensational spectacle of Aurora Australis or the Southern Lights, the southern hemisphere's answer to its northern counterpart. Dances of greens, blues, and violets illuminate the polar nights, providing a spectacular display, visible only from the most southerly latitudes.

By connecting these hidden geographies across the continents, we hope to infuse travelers with a sense of wonder, tell untold stories, and foster an appreciation for the diversity of environment and human ingenuity the world has to offer. From untouched wildernesses to quaint villages, hidden beaches to isolated ruins, the world is filled with innumerable hidden gems, waiting to be discovered by the culturally curious. Go beyond the familiar, venture into the unknown, and you might just discover places that touch your soul in a way you never expected.

Chapter 8. Negotiating the Labyrinth of Social Norms

Navigating the social norms of new cultures can often feel like finding your way through an intricate labyrinth. It weaves the complex, yet invisible web of society that dictates behavior and consideration. These norms vary from culture to culture, and knowing the nuances becomes essential to cultivate meaningful relationships and partake in authentic experiences.

8.1. Understanding Social Norms

Before stepping into the maze, it is important to comprehend the essence of social norms. These are the guidelines that dictate what is deemed acceptable behavior within any given society, ranging from everyday etiquettes, like how to greet someone, to more complex issues like gender roles or religious observances. Social norms are born out of a culture's history, environment, and the shared beliefs of its people. They encapsulate the core values of any society and serve as the blueprint for interactions.

8.2. Acquiring Cultural Knowledge

Learning and understanding social norms begins with acquiring cultural knowledge before and during travel. It is not enough to simply step off the plane and hope to blend in. It begins with diligent research on the destination and its customs. Guide books can be excellent resources for this, as can documentaries, films, and even local literature. Conversing with locals, either virtually or in-person, can provide an authentic and insightful view of cultural norms. Encouraging curiosity about social norms should be an integral part of your travel preparation, echoing the mantra, "When in Rome, do as the Romans do".

8.3. The Importance of Observance

Once you've gathered ample knowledge about the destination, observance becomes key. It's essential to be mindful of actions, words, and even body language when interacting with locals. Observing locals in different situations can provide a real-life example of how these social norms are enacted, providing you with a model to emulate. Immersion is key, as it allows you to develop a deeper understanding of the intricacies of these norms.

8.4. Navigating Conflict

Even with the most intensive preparation, conflicts due to misunderstandings may arise. The key factor when faced with such conflicts is to remain respectful and understanding. Realize that offending someone because of cultural ignorance is a mistake, but persisting in wrong behavior after learning it's incorrect can be taken as disrespectful. Apologize sincerely when a mistake is made, and most importantly, learn from it. This not only shows the individual you've offended that you respect their culture and feelings, but also serves as a warning to avoid similar missteps in the future.

8.5. The Linguistic Element

Language barriers can be formidable opponents in negotiating social norms. While learning the entirety of a new language might not be feasible, understanding some key phrases and expressions can be tremendously helpful. Many societies have social norms built around certain phrases, greetings, or expressions. Grasping these can be of immense help in breaking the ice and connecting deeply with locals.

8.6. The Art of Respect

Above all, respect for the sensitivities and rules of a different culture is essential. You're a guest in their homeland, and adhering to social norms is a sign of respect – not just for individuals but for the entire culture and its history. This respect, in turn, ensures that the attitude toward you is respectful, too, opening doors onto experiences that might otherwise remain closed.

8.7. Lessons Learnt and Unlearned

Traveling often challenges preconceived notions and biases about different cultures. Recognizing this and questioning your own assumptions is a critical part of understanding social norms. You unlearn and relearn things, bringing about personal growth and a better appreciation for the diversity of human cultures. It's an enlightening journey as you negotiate the labyrinth of social norms, and the reward at the end is a richer, more vibrant experience of the world.

8.8. The Grand Takeaway

Travel doesn't just broaden your geographical understanding; it broadens your cultural horizons and disrupts your perception of societal norms. Embrace the labyrinth of social norms as an enlightening journey, for it is not about finding an exit. The real breakthrough comes when you find your way deeper into the culture, blending so effortlessly that the lines between you, the traveler, and the local blur, leading to a unique sense of belonging and richer experiences. In this jigsaw puzzle of global cultures, each piece is colored with its unique norms, making your journey truly vibrant.

In a world increasingly characterized by globalization, it's the understanding and implementation of these social norms that bridge the gap between cultures, fostering a sense of unity in diversity. Your tour around the world, thus, is not merely harvesting experiences but also sowing the richness of cultural respect and understanding.

Chapter 9. Making Connections: From Being a Tourist to a Local

Our esteemed reader, we invite you now to delve deep into one of the most rewarding aspects of travel - the transformation from being a mere tourist to feeling as though you are truly part of the local culture. We aim to provide you with valuable insights and concrete steps toward accomplishing this transformation, focusing on thoughtful interaction, seeking out immersive experiences, and developing an active interest in the nuances of local traditions and customs.

9.1. Forming Genuine Relationships

Often, the journey from casual vacationer to an engaged local begins with forming genuine relationships. These relationships may range from a fleeting conversation with your taxi driver to a long-term friendship with a local guide. Each interaction is an opportunity to learn and grow. An earnest willingness to engage will open doors to stunning experiences beyond what you might find online or in guidebooks.

It's essential to respect the other individual during these interactions. Respect their time, their stories, and their way of life. Abrupt, self-interested encounters are the antithesis of meaningful connections. Ask questions, be curious, but show consideration and always remember the golden rule - treat others how you want to be treated.

9.2. Embracing Local Culture and Traditions

Locals are the custodians of the rich tapestry of culture and traditions that make a destination unique. Show an active interest in their festivals, local lore, traditions, and even daily routines. You might want to learn how to dance the flamenco in Spain, understand the symbolism of Balinese Hindu rituals, or know the significance of tea in Chinese culture. Adopt the stance of a learner, open your mind to new experiences, embrace the unfamiliar, and find joy in these enlightening pursuits.

9.3. Mastering the Local Language

Language conveys more than words; it speaks volumes about a culture's history and way of thinking. While it's not feasible for you to become fluent in many different languages each time you travel, learning a few basic phrases can make a world of difference. Simple words such as "hello," "thank you," and "please" show respect and eagerness to engage, helping bridge gaps and create bonds. You will notice locals light up when you attempt to communicate in their tongue, demonstrating your respect for their culture and traditions.

9.4. Discovering Local Cuisine

Trying local food is an immersive experience that goes far beyond sating your hunger. Local dishes are the culmination of centuries of culture and tradition. In India, for instance, food varies dramatically from one region to another, reflecting local populations' diversity. In Italy, you will find traditional recipes passed down through generations, each carrying an essence of the land and the love of a Nonna. Dine at local eateries or, better still, arrange cooking lessons to learn, bond, and engage over delicious food.

9.5. Participating Actively in Local Events

Local events and festivals provide a delightful platform for immersing oneself in local culture. Whether it's attending the luminous lantern festival in Thailand or participating in the coffee harvesting traditions in Colombia – these unique experiences often evolve into unforgettable memories. It's beneficial to research local events before the trip and be open to unexpected happenings during your stay.

Transforming from a tourist to a de facto local takes time and can't be rushed. The process is one of uncertainty, learning, and many unexpected revelations. As you continue your journey through different parts of the world, navigate this path with genuine intent, patience, and open-mindedness. These qualities will help you form meaningful connections, transform into an integrated part of the local scene, and ultimately enrich the travel experience.

Chapter 10. Responsible Travel: Nurturing the Cultural Heritage

Travel, by its very nature, is a transformative experience. It heralds change, not just within the traveler, but within the host communities as well. However, the consequences of our travels are not always beneficial. Often times, without adequate understanding and care, the cultural heritage that attracts us to certain destinations gets eroded due to unchecked or irresponsible tourism acts. This chapter is designed to guide you, dear reader, on the path of responsible travel by nurturing and preserving the rich tapestry of cultural heritage across our globe.

10.1. Exploring the Concept of Cultural Heritage

Cultural heritage is an intricate concept. It embodies the physical artifacts and tangible creations, like buildings or landscapes, that are inherited from past generations, maintained in the present and passed on to future generations. But cultural heritage is not solely composed of brick, mortar, or artifacts. It also thrives in the intangible: narratives, customs, cuisine, rituals, songs, and knowledge.

This broad spectrum of cultural heritage presents a vibrant tableau for the traveler. From the Pyramids of Egypt to the songs of South America's indigenous tribes; from the bustling markets of Marrakech to the tranquil temple rituals of Japan - these poignant experiences have shaped humanity's past, and will continue to form our future. Yet, it is this very allure of cultural heritage that makes it vulnerable.

10.2. The Impact of Travel on Cultural Heritage

The exciting journey that tourism presents poses significant risks to preserving cultural heritage. Critical aspects are highlighted below:

1. The exploitation of cultural heritage: This occurs when important cultural symbols, artifacts, or customs are commodified for tourism, often altering their narrative, authenticity or significance.

2. Mass tourism: High volumes of tourists can lead to the physical erosion of heritage sites, undermining their longevity.

3. Cultural insensitivity: Ignorance about or negligence towards local customs and traditions can result in offending the host communities, damaging the cultural fabric. These challenges highlight the dire need to foster a sense of responsibility among travelers to ensure the preservation of cultural heritage.

10.3. The Role of Responsible Travel in Nurturing Cultural Heritage

Responsible travel requires balancing our desire for exploration with the need to respect, preserve, and nurture the cultures we visit. Here are some thoughts on how we can achieve this:

1. Education and Awareness: Knowledge is the key to mutual understanding and respect. Gain an understanding of the local customs and traditions of your destination prior to arrival.

2. Patronize local businesses: This aids in sustaining the local economy and tepidly keeping age-old traditions alive.

3. Follow guidelines and rules: Respect the limits set by authorities at heritage sites. This helps in reducing the risk of damage.

4. Foster Cultural Interactions: Engage directly with locals, understanding their view of their heritage.

5. Minimize your footprint: From reducing waste to lowering carbon emissions, doing your part for the environment also helps safeguard a locality's cultural heritage.

10.4. Walking the Talk

Now let us turn these principles into action. Start by becoming an informed traveler. Seek out reputable sources of information about your destination's culture, traditions, and norms. Invest in local businesses by choosing local services and products. When visiting heritage sites, remember the 'leave no trace' principle – take only photographs, leave only footprints. Engage respectfully with locals, delving into their narratives and wisdom, becoming a guardian of their shared stories. Minimize waste, use public transport, and try to offset carbon emissions associated with your travel.

10.5. Nurturing and Preserving for the Future

Advances in technology and increasing interconnectedness will continue to open up remote corners of the world for exploration. As custodians of cultural heritage, it is incumbent upon us to ensure these explorations nurture rather than erode these priceless assets. Only then shall the future generations revel in the rich tapestry of mankind's past. This journey shall require continuous learning, adaptation, and respect for the myriad cultures that dot our planet.

By bearing the mantle of responsible tourism, we not only safeguard humanity's cultural heritage but also enrich our travel experience, fostering a deeper connection to the people and places we visit.

And thus, the journey continues, not as a fleeting tourist, but as a respectful traveler – a traveler who understands that his or her footprints on foreign soil can either lead to the nurturing of cultural heritage or to its unfortunate degradation. Let us all aim to leave a positive, lasting legacy behind on every journey we embark upon. Let us harbor the desire to nurture, protect, and relish the remarkable cultural heritage that our world has to offer.

Travel is more than just seeing the sights; it is a deep and enriching engagement with the world's diverse cultures, traditions, and histories. When we comprehend the implications of our travels and take steps to make them responsible, we create a symbiotic relationship with our host cultures, one that nurtures and enriches both sides. So let us tread lightly, respectfully, and thoughtfully, bearing in mind that the world's cultural heritage is a treasure that needs to be safeguarded diligently for generations to come. And on that note, we conclude our detailed exploration into responsible travel and the nurturing of cultural heritage.

Chapter 11. Looking Ahead: The Future of Culturally Curious Travel

As we stand on the precipice of the future, we can imagine the exciting changes that culturally curious travel will undergo. Advances in technology, increasing cognizance about culture, and chronicling of previously unexplored terrains - all promise to transform the face of this unique form of wanderlust. Yet at the same time, we reckon with a rapidly changing global environment and grapple with the question of how we can travel responsibly, all while augmenting our enrichment through global cultures.

11.1. Interactions with Technology

The integration of advancements in technology with culturally curious travel promises to elevate experiential journeying to another plane. Revolutionary tech such as virtual reality and augmented reality show immense promise in recreating immersive travel experiences. Imagine strolling through the bustling mercado of San Miguel de Allende or walking bedside a procession in Indian pre-historic ruins - all from the comfort of your home. Alternatively, AR could provide essential cultural, historical, and logistical information during an authentic on-site exploration, thereby enriching your travel experience.

Artificial Intelligence is set to contribute in numerous ways, most notably in terms of language translation which can facilitate smoother and richer cultural communication. Machine learning has the potential to curate highly personalized experiences based on your preferences, from local customs and traditions to the indigenous cuisine best suited to your palate. Unquestionably, the technology will be an instrumental tool to connect, understand, and appreciate diverse cultures in a much deeper sense.

11.2. Embracing Globalism

People around the world are increasingly recognizing the immense wealth that global cultures carry. As our curiosity to understand, respect, and celebrate them grows, so does our desire to encounter them in their truest forms. If this trend of embracing globalism continues, we may expect to see unparalleled interest and participation in local festivals, cultural events, and traditional practices around the world.

This enthusiasm is likely to spur the growth of micro-tourism, where travelers will favor immersing themselves in specific localities or communities, experiencing their culture, food, and traditions to the fullest. Sustainable tourism, where travel is tied to supporting local businesses and preserving the cultural heritage rather than exploiting resources, is likely to see a significant growth spurt.

11.3. Uncharted Terrains

There has been a renewed interest in uncharted terrains, primarily due to digital characterization of remote areas, and in part because of mankind's insatiable curiosity. As sophisticated modes of transport and infrastructure development make the farthest reaches of the globe accessible, we may find that these off-the-beaten-path destinations become hotspots for culturally curious travelers. The opportunity to meet local communities — appreciate their unique rituals, art forms, and delicacies, and engage in dialogues about their way of life — will offer an enriching travel experience that is to be found nowhere else.

11.4. Responsibly Curious

Given the mounting concerns about the environmental impact of tourism, the future of culturally curious travel mandates a significant shift towards sustainable practices. Travelers are increasingly realizing the importance of responsible tourism – making every journey matter not only as a personal experience but also as a contributor to the socio-cultural and economic health of the host communities. This includes looking out for and giving precedence to eco-friendly accommodations, availing locally made items and services over mass-produced goods, and ensuring that local customs and sensibilities are respected.

Additionally, the potential impact of mass tourism on fragile cultural heritages cannot be understated. Hence, the future traveler should be well educated and aware to avoid interfering unduly with local vibes and traditions. Respecting the life and rhythm of the local community should emerge as a non-negotiable tenet of travel.

As we step into the future teeming with endless possibilities, being culturally curious will mean continually adapting and learning. It will mean harnessing technology to augment our experiences rather than let it overshadow the culture we seek. It will mean upholding tradition while respecting our environment, and seeking new knowledge while retaining our empowering, acquired wisdom. The future of culturally curious travel necessitates that we journey forward, not just in distance, but in awareness, understanding, and respect. Ultimately, the journey will be about making the world a little more familiar, one culture at a time.

www.ingramcontent.com/pod-product-compliance
Lightning Source LLC
Chambersburg PA
CBHW071050260726
48661CB00007B/3235